THE SHOUT

THE SHOUT

Selected Poems

Simon Armitage

ALFRED A. KNOPF   NEW YORK   2012

THIS IS A BORZOI BOOK
PUBLISHED BY ALFRED A. KNOPF

Published in the United States by Alfred A. Knopf, a division of
Random House, Inc., New York. Originally published in hardcover
by Houghton Mifflin Harcourt Publishing Company, Boston, in 2005.

www.aaknopf.com

The poems in this work were previously published in the following
collections: *The Dead Sea* (London: Faber & Faber, 1995); *Moon
Country* by Simon Armitage and Glyn Maxwell (London: Faber &
Faber, 1996); *CloudCuckooLand* (London: Faber & Faber, 1997); *Book
of Matches* (London: Faber & Faber, 2001); *The Universal Home Doctor*
(London: Faber & Faber, 2002); *Tyrannosaurus Rex Versus the
Corduroy Kid* (London: Faber & Faber, 2006, and New York:
Alfred A. Knopf, 2008).

Library of Congress Cataloging-in-Publication Data
Armitage, Simon, 1963–
The shout : selected poems / Simon Armitage.—1st ed.
p.   cm.
"This is a Borzoi book."
"Originally published by Harcourt in 2005."
ISBN 978-0-375-71206-7
I. Title.
PR6051.R564A6 2012
821'.914—dc22   2012003210

Jacket design by Carol Devine Carson
Manufactured in the United States of America
First Paperback Edition

CONTENTS

THE SHOUT

THE SHOUT

We went out
into the school yard together, me and the boy
whose name and face

I don't remember. We were testing the range
of the human voice:
he had to shout for all he was worth,

I had to raise an arm
from across the divide to signal back
that the sound had carried.

He called from over the park—I lifted an arm.
Out of bounds,
he yelled from the end of the road,

from the foot of the hill,
from beyond the look-out post of Fretwell's Farm—
I lifted an arm.

He left town, went on to be twenty years dead
with a gunshot hole
in the roof of his mouth, in Western Australia.

Boy with the name and face I don't remember,
you can stop shouting now, I can still hear you.

GOOSEBERRY SEASON

Which reminds me. He appeared
at noon, asking for water. He'd walked from town
after losing his job, leaving a note for his wife and his brother
and locking his dog in the coal bunker.
We made him a bed

and he slept till Monday.
A week went by and he hung up his coat.
Then a month, and not a stroke of work, a word of thanks,
a farthing of rent or a sign of him leaving.
One evening he mentioned a recipe

for smooth, seedless gooseberry sorbet
but by then I was tired of him: taking pocket money
from my boy at cards, sucking up to my wife and on his last
    night
sizing up my daughter. He was smoking my pipe
as we stirred his supper.

Where does the hand become the wrist?
Where does the neck become the shoulder? The watershed
and then the weight, whatever turns up and tips us over that
    razor's edge
between something and nothing, between
one and the other.

I could have told him this
but didn't bother. We ran him a bath
and held him under, dried him off and dressed him
and loaded him into the back of the pick-up.
Then we drove without headlights

to the county boundary,
dropped the tailgate, and after my boy
had been through his pockets we dragged him like a mattress
across the meadow and on the count of four
threw him over the border.

This is not general knowledge, except
in gooseberry season, which reminds me, and at the table
I have been known to raise an eyebrow, or scoop the sorbet
into five equal portions, for the hell of it.
I mention this for a good reason.

AT SEA

It is not through weeping,
but all evening the pale blue eye
on your most photogenic side has kept
its own unfathomable tide. Like the boy
at the dyke I have been there:

held out a huge finger,
lifted atoms of dust with the point
of a tissue and imagined slivers of hair
in the oil on the cornea. We are both
in the dark, but I go on

drawing the eyelid up by its lashes,
folding it almost inside-out, then finding
and hiding every mirror in the house
as the iris, besieged with the ink
of blood rolls back

into its own orbit. Nothing
will help it. Through until dawn
you dream the true story of the boy
who hooked out his eye and ate it,
so by six in the morning

I am steadying the ointment
that will bite like an onion, piping
a line of cream while avoiding the pupil
and in no time it is glued shut
like a bad mussel.

Friends call round
and mean well. They wait
and whisper in the air-lock of the lobby
with patches, eyewash, the truth
about mascara.

Even the cats are onto it;
they bring in starlings, and because their feathers
are the colours of oil on water in sunlight
they are a sign of something.
In the long hours

beyond us, irritations heal
into arguments. For the eighteenth time
it comes to this: the length of your leg sliding out
from the covers, the ball of your foot
like a fist on the carpet

while downstairs
I cannot bring myself to hear it.
Words have been spoken; things that were bottled
have burst open and to walk in now
would be to walk in

on the ocean.

POEM

And if it snowed and snow covered the drive
he took a spade and tossed it to one side.
And always tucked his daughter up at night.
And slippered her the one time that she lied.

And every week he tipped up half his wage.
And what he didn't spend each week he saved.
And praised his wife for every meal she made.
And once, for laughing, punched her in the face.

And for his mum he hired a private nurse.
And every Sunday taxied her to church.
And he blubbed when she went from bad to worse.
And twice he lifted ten quid from her purse.

Here's how they rated him when they looked back:
sometimes he did this, sometimes he did that.

KID

Batman, big shot, when you gave the order
to grow up, then let me loose to wander
leeward, freely through the wild blue yonder
as you liked to say, or ditched me, rather,
in the gutter . . . well, I turned the corner.
Now I've scotched that "he was like a father
to me" rumour, sacked it, blown the cover
on that "he was like an elder brother"
story, let the cat out on that caper
with the married woman, how you took her
downtown on expenses in the motor.
Holy robin-redbreast-nest-egg-shocker!
Holy roll-me-over-in-the-clover,
I'm not playing ball boy any longer
Batman, now I've doffed that off-the-shoulder
Sherwood-Forest-green and scarlet number
for a pair of jeans and crew-neck jumper;
now I'm taller, harder, stronger, older.
Batman, it makes a marvellous picture:
you without a shadow, stewing over
chicken giblets in the pressure cooker,
next to nothing in the walk-in larder,
punching the palm of your hand all winter,
you baby, now I'm the real boy wonder.

LINES THOUGHT TO HAVE BEEN WRITTEN ON THE EVE OF THE EXECUTION OF A WARRANT FOR HIS ARREST

Boys, I have a feeling in my water,
in my bones, that should we lose our houses
and our homes, our jobs, or just in general
come unstuck, she will not lend one button
from her blouse, and from her kitchen garden
not one bean. But through farmyards and dust bowls
we will lay down our topcoats, or steel ourselves
and bare our backs over streams and manholes.

Down Birdcage Walk in riots or wartime
we will not hear of her hitching her skirt
or see for ourselves that frantic footwork,
busy like a swan's beneath the surface.
But quickly our tank will stop in its tracks;
they'll turn the turret lid back like a stone;
inside, our faces set like flint, her name
cross-threaded in the barrels of our throats.

I have this from reliable sources:
boys, with our letters, our first class honours
and diplomas we are tenfold brighter
than her sons and daughters put together.
But someone hangs on every word they speak,
and let me mention here the hummingbird
that seems suspended at the orchid's lips,
or else the bird that picks the hippo's teeth.

Boys, if we burn, she will not pass one drop
of water over us, and if we drown
she will not let a belt or bootlace down,
or lend a hand. She'll turn instead and show
a leg, a stocking, sheer and ladderless.
And even then we will not lose our heads
by mouthing an air bubble out of turn
or spouting a smoke ring against her name.

But worse than this, in handouts and speeches
she will care for us, and cannot mean it.
Picture the stroke of the hour that takes her:
our faces will freeze as if the wind had changed,
we shall hear in our hearts a note, a murmur,
and talk in terms of where we stood, how struck,
how still we were the moment this happened,
in good faith, as if it really mattered.

NOT THE FURNITURE GAME

His hair was a crow fished out of a blocked chimney
and his eyes were boiled eggs with the tops hammered in
and his blink was a cat flap
and his teeth were bluestones or Easter Island statues
and his bite was a perfect horseshoe.
His nostrils were both barrels of a shotgun, loaded.
And his mouth was an oil exploration project gone bankrupt
and his last smile was a caesarean section
and his tongue was an iguanodon
and his whistle was a laser beam
and his laugh was a bad case of kennel cough.
He coughed, and it was malt whisky.
And his headaches were Arson in Her Majesty's Dockyards
and his arguments were outboard motors strangled with
        fishing-line
and his neck was a bandstand
and his Adam's apple was a ball cock
and his arms were milk running off from a broken bottle.
His elbows were boomerangs or pinking shears.
And his wrists were ankles
and his handshakes were puff adders in the bran tub
and his fingers were astronauts found dead in their spacesuits
and the palms of his hands were action paintings
and both thumbs were blue touchpaper.
And his shadow was an opencast mine.
And his dog was a sentry-box with no one in it
and his heart was a first world war grenade discovered by
        children
and his nipples were timers for incendiary devices

and his shoulder blades were two butchers at the
        meat-cleaving competition
and his belly-button was the Falkland Islands
and his private parts were the Bermuda Triangle
and his backside was a priest hole
and his stretchmarks were the tide going out.
The whole system of his blood was Dutch elm disease.
And his legs were depth charges
and his knees were fossils waiting to be tapped open
and his ligaments were rifles wrapped in oilcloth under the
        floorboards
and his calves were the undercarriages of Shackletons.
The balls of his feet were where meteorites had landed
and his toes were a nest of mice under the lawn-mower.
And his footprints were Vietnam
and his promises were hot-air balloons floating off over
        the trees
and his one-liners were footballs through other people's
        windows
and his grin was the Great Wall of China as seen from
        the moon
and the last time they talked, it was apartheid.

She was a chair, tipped over backwards
with his donkey jacket on her shoulders.

They told him,
and his face was a hole
where the ice had not been thick enough to hold her.

ROBINSON IN TWO CITIES

Cities of architecture and scaffolding, tower blocks
taking the temperature, external elevator-cars outpacing
window-cleaning cages, projects and broken deadlines,
    Robinson

near the station. All routes end here. Cities of junctions
and ring roads, inside lanes peeling off to the left
shunting traffic into neighbourhoods, districts, Robinson

on the loop bus, his third lap. Cranes making the skyline.
Cities of offences against the person, taxis and sirens
and crossing the street from nowhere to nowhere, Robinson

on foot. Cities at dusk, each outpointing the other
with starlings. A choice of evening papers, the bridge,
and later with his tightrope act along the ledge, Robinson

in two minds.

THE LOST LETTER OF THE LATE JUD FRY

Wake.
And in my head
walk barefoot, naked from the bed
towards the day, then
wait.

Hold.
The dawn will crack
its egg into the morning's bowl
and him on horseback,
gold.

Me,
I'm in the shed, I'm
working on it: a plus b plus c, it's
you, him, me. It's
three.

Hell,
this hole, this shack.
The sun makes light of me
behind my back.
Well,

good.
I give you the applause
of ringdoves lifting from the wood
and, for an encore,
blood.

Look,
see, no man
should be me, the very opposite
of snowman:
soot.

I
work that black dust
where I slice your name into my forearm
with a jackknife: L.A.U.R.E.
Y.

You
at the window now,
undressed. I underestimated him,
never saw you as a pair, a
two.

Yours—
that's him for sure.
The sun will have its day,
its weeks, months,
years.

Fine.
But just for once, for me,
dig deep, think twice, be otherwise, be
someone else this time.
Mine.

TO POVERTY
(after Laycock)

You are near again, and have been there
or thereabouts for years. Pull up a chair.
I'd know that shadow anywhere, that silhouette
without a face, that shape. Well, be my guest.
We'll live like sidekicks—hip to hip,
like Siamese twins, joined at the pocket.

I've tried too long to see the back of you.
Last winter when you came down with the flu
I should have split, cut loose, but
let you pass the buck, the bug. Bad blood.
It's cold again; come closer to the fire, the light,
and let me make you out.

How have you hurt me, let me count the ways:
the months of Sundays
when you left me in the damp, the dark,
the red, or down and out, or out of work.
The weeks on end of bread without butter,
bed without supper.

That time I fell through Schofield's shed
and broke both legs,
and Schofield couldn't spare to split
one stick of furniture to make a splint.
Thirteen weeks I sat there till they set.
What can the poor do but wait? And wait.

How come you're struck with me? Go see the Queen,
lean on the doctor or the dean,
breathe on the major,
squeeze the mason or the manager,
go down to London, find a novelist at least
to bother with, to bleed, to leech.

On second thoughts, stay put.
A person needs to get a person close enough
to stab him in the back.
Robert Frost said that. Besides,
I'd rather keep you in the corner of my eye
than wait for you to join me side by side
at every turn, on every street, in every town.
Sit down. I said sit down.

PARABLE OF THE DEAD DONKEY

Instructions arrived by registered post
under cover of separate envelopes:
directions first
to pinpoint the place
in the shape of maps and compass bearings;
those, then forms and stamps for loss of earnings.
So much was paid
to diggers of graves
by keepers or next of kin, peg leg
(which made for the dumping of quadrupeds):
sixteen quid
to send off a pig
or sink a pit for a dog or pony.
But less to plant a man than a donkey.
Cheaper by half
for a pregnant horse
that died with all four hooves inside her
than one with a stillborn foal beside her.
And this was a bind,
being duty bound
where ownership was unestablished.
We filled the flasks and loaded the Transit,
then set out, making
for the undertaking.

Facing north, he was dead at three o'clock
in a ring of meadow grass, closely cropped,
where a metal chain
on a wooden stake
had stopped him ambling off at an angle,

worn him down in a perfect circle.
We burrowed in
right next to him
through firm white soil. An hour's hard labour
took us five feet down—and then the weather:
thunder biting
the heels of lightning,
a cloudburst drawing a curtain of rain
across us, filling the bath of the grave,
and we waded in it
for one more minute,
dredged and shovelled as the tide was rising,
bailed out for fear of drowning, capsizing.
Back on top
we weighed him up,
gave some thought to this beast of the Bible:
the nose and muzzle, the teeth, the eyeballs,
the rump, the hindquarters,
the flanks, the shoulders,
everything soothed in the oil of the rain—
the eel of his tongue, the keel of his spine,
the rope of his tail,
the weeds of his mane.
Then we turned him about and slipped his anchor,
eased him out of the noose of his tether,
and rolled him in
and started to dig.
But even with donkey, water and soil
there wasn't enough to level the hole
after what was washed away
or turned into clay
or trodden in, so we opened the earth
and started in on a second trench for dirt

to fill the first.
Which left a taste
of starting something that wouldn't finish:
a covered grave with a donkey in it,
a donkey-size hole
within a stone's throw
and not a single bone to drop in it
or a handful of dust to toss on top of it.

The van wouldn't start, so we wandered home
on foot, in the dark, without supper or profit.

HITCHER

I'd been tired, under
the weather, but the ansaphone kept screaming:
One more sick-note, mister, and you're finished. Fired.
I thumbed a lift to where the car was parked.
A Vauxhall Astra. It was hired.

I picked him up in Leeds.
He was following the sun to west from east
with just a toothbrush and the good earth for a bed. The truth,
he said, was blowin' in the wind,
or round the next bend.

I let him have it
on the top road out of Harrogate—once
with the head, then six times with the krooklok
in the face—and didn't even swerve.
I dropped it into third

and leant across
to let him out, and saw him in the mirror
bouncing off the kerb, then disappearing down the verge.
We were the same age, give or take a week.
He'd said he liked the breeze

to run its fingers
through his hair. It was twelve noon.
The outlook for the day was moderate to fair.
Stitch that, I remember thinking,
you can walk from there.

TO HIS LOST LOVER

Now they are no longer
any trouble to each other

he can turn things over, get down to that list
of things that never happened, all of the lost

unfinishable business.
For instance . . . for instance,

how he never clipped and kept her hair, or drew a hairbrush
through that style of hers, and never knew how not to blush

at the fall of her name in close company.
How they never slept like buried cutlery—

two spoons or forks cupped perfectly together,
or made the most of some heavy weather—

walked out into hard rain under sheet lightning,
or did the gears while the other was driving.

How he never raised his fingertips
to stop the segments of her lips

from breaking the news,
or tasted the fruit,

or picked for himself the pear of her heart,
or lifted her hand to where his own heart

was a small, dark, terrified bird
in her grip. Where it hurt.

Or said the right thing,
or put it in writing.

And never fled the black mile back to his house
before midnight, or coaxed another button of her blouse,

then another,
or knew her

favourite colour,
her taste, her flavour,

and never ran a bath or held a towel for her,
or soft-soaped her, or whipped her hair

into an ice-cream cornet or a beehive
of lather, or acted out of turn, or misbehaved

when he might have, or worked a comb
where no comb had been, or walked back home

through a black mile hugging a punctured heart,
where it hurt, where it hurt, or helped her hand

to his butterfly heart
in its two blue halves.

And never almost cried,
and never once described

an attack of the heart,
or under a silk shirt

nursed in his hand her breast,
her left, like a tear of flesh

wept by the heart,
where it hurts,

or brushed with his thumb the nut of her nipple,
or drank intoxicating liquors from her navel.

Or christened the Pole Star in her name,
or shielded the mask of her face like a flame,

a pilot light,
or stayed the night,

or steered her back to that house of his,
or said "Don't ask me to say how it is

I like you.
I just might do."

How he never figured out a fireproof plan,
or unravelled her hand, as if her hand

were a solid ball
of silver foil

and discovered a lifeline hiding inside it,
and measured the trace of his own alongside it.

But said some things and never meant them—
sweet nothings anybody could have mentioned.

And left unsaid some things he should have spoken,
about the heart, where it hurt exactly, and how often.

MR. ROBINSON'S HOLIDAY

As if gravity had brought him here, down
through the matrix of the minor counties
to the South West where the mainland dips its toe
in the ocean. From the cliff, with the viewfinder,

Robinson trained on a seal in the bay coming up
like a spaceman. And in the guesthouse,
Robinson giving a bogus address, not wanting
the landlord's friends to visit his place, force

the window casements, try on his wardrobe
in the full-length mirror, load up with photographs
and tapes or help themselves to a cooked breakfast.
Robinson thinking this is ridiculous, Robinson.

One word about the weather: uncertain. One sock
in his coat pocket, that's odd, and for the upkeep
of this private shore, Robinson slotting a hermit crab
in the honesty-box. Time on his hands:

Robinson at the beach, baking slowly like a loaf
for hours, shaking down behind the windbreak,
then all evening finding sand running out
from unlikely places. The mark where his watch was—

a good day's work, Robinson. As for St. Michael's Mount
he would rather die than pay the ferryman, and
in the hour before high tide on the flooded causeway—
Robinson ghost-like and up to his neck in it.

Look, it is overwhelming; the air at St. Ives
so good he could take a slice and frame it,
and this the town where the smell of fish
once stopped a clock. Robinson not one

for taking things lightly, not one for caution
on those roller-coasting lanes over the coves and inlets.
Robinson's radio—good news on the weather front:
sunshine mainly with bulletins of rain.

At the stately home, his boots impounded for a pair
of plastic overshoes, then warned for touching this
and brushing that and nudging the other. Robinson
to himself: unclean, unclean. Back at the room,

Robinson damned if he'll pay an extra pound
for a plug for the bath, soaking for an hour at least
with his heel in the hole. Then without a towel
drying off on the curtain. Typical, Robinson. Typical.

Awake all night, a man in the next room coughing
like a seal. Down on the shore the moon like a torch;
whichever way he walks it finds him, follows him,
will not flinch when he spins round to surprise it,

and in that way reminds him.

THE DEAD SEA POEMS

And I was travelling lightly, barefoot
over bedrock, then through lands that were stitched
with breadplant and camomile. Or was it

burdock? For a living I was driving
a river of goats towards clean water,
when one of the herd cut loose to a cave

on the skyline. To flush it out, I shaped
a sling from a length of cotton bandage,
or was it a blanket, then launched a rock

at the target, which let out a racket—
the tell-tale sound of man-made objects.
Inside the cave like a set of skittles

stood a dozen caskets, and each one gasped—
a little theatrically perhaps—
when opened, then gave out a breath of musk

and pollen, and reaching down through cool sand
I found poems written in my own hand.
Being greatly in need of food and clothing,

and out of pocket, I let the lot go
for twelve times nothing, but saw them again
this spring, on public display, out of reach

under infrared and ultrasonic,
apparently worth an absolute packet.
Knowing now the price of my early art

I have gone some way towards taking it all
to heart, by bearing it all in mind, like
praying, saying it over and over

at night, by singing the whole of the work
to myself, every page of that innocent,
everyday, effortless verse, of which this

is the first.

MAN WITH A GOLF BALL HEART

They set about him with a knife and fork, I heard,
and spooned it out. Dunlop, dimpled, perfectly hard.
It bounced on stone but not on softer ground—they made
a note of that. They slit the skin—a leathery,
rubbery, eyelid thing—and further in, three miles
of gut or string, elastic. Inside that, a pouch
or sac of pearl-white balm or gloss, like Copydex.
It weighed in at the low end of the litmus test
but wouldn't burn, and tasted bitter, bad, resin
perhaps from a tree or plant. And it gave off gas
that caused them all to weep when they inspected it.

That heart had been an apple once, they reckoned. Green.
They had a scheme to plant an apple there again
beginning with a pip, but he rejected it.

I SAY I SAY I SAY

Anyone here had a go at themselves
for a laugh? Anyone opened their wrists
with a blade in the bath? Those in the dark
at the back, listen hard. Those at the front
in the know, those of us who have, hands up,
let's show that inch of lacerated skin
between the forearm and the fist. Let's tell it
like it is: strong drink, a crimson tidemark
round the tub, a yard of lint, white towels
washed a dozen times, still pink. Tough luck.
A passion then for watches, bangles, cuffs.
A likely story: you were lashed by brambles
picking berries from the woods. Come clean, come good,
repeat with me the punch line "Just like blood"
when those at the back rush forward to say
how a little love goes a long long long way.

WHITE CHRISTMAS

For once it is a white Christmas,
so white the roads are impassable
and my wife is snowbound
in a town untroubled by tractor or snowplough.
In bed, awake, alone. She calls

and we pass on our presents by telephone.
Mine is a watch, the very one
I would have chosen. Hers is a song,
the one with the line *Here come the hills of time*
and it sits in its sleeve,

unsung and unopened. But the dog downstairs
is worrying, gnawing, howling,
so I walk her through clean snow
along the tow-path to the boat-house at a steady pace,
then to my parents' place

where my mother is Marie Curie, in the kitchen
discovering radium, and my father is Fred Flintstone,
and a guest from the past has a look on her face meaning
lie and I'll have your teeth for a necklace, boy,
your eyeballs for earrings,

your bullshit for breakfast,
and my two-year-old niece is baby Jesus,
passing between us with the fruit of the earth
and the light of the world—Christingle—a blood orange
spiked with a burning candle.

We eat, but the dog begs at the table,
drinks from the toilet, sings in the cellar.
Only baby Jesus wanders with me down the stairs
with a shank of meat to see her, to feed her.
Later, when I stand to leave

my father wants to shake me by the hand
but my arms are heavy, made of a base metal,
and the dog wants to take me down the black lane, back
to an empty house again. A car goes by
with my sister inside

and to wave goodnight
she lifts the arm of the sleeping infant Christ,
but I turn my wrist to notice the time. There and then
I'm the man in the joke, the man in a world of friends
where all the clocks are stopped,

synchronising his own watch.

BEFORE YOU CUT LOOSE,

                                        put dogs on the list
of difficult things to lose. Those dogs ditched
on the North York Moors or the Sussex Downs
or hurled like bags of sand from rented cars
have followed their noses to market towns
and bounced like balls into their owners' arms.
I heard one story of a dog that swam
to the English coast from the Isle of Man,
and a dog that carried eggs and bacon
and a morning paper from the village
surfaced umpteen leagues and two years later,
bacon eaten but the eggs unbroken,
newsprint dry as tinder, to the letter.
A dog might wander the width of the map
to bury its head in its owner's lap,
crawl the last mile to dab a bleeding paw
against its own front door. To die at home,
a dog might walk its four legs to the bone.
You can take off the tag and the collar
but a dog wears one coat and one colour.
A dog got rid of—that's a dog for life.
No dog howls like a dog kicked out at night.
Try looking a dog like that in the eye.

GOALKEEPER WITH A CIGARETTE

That's him in the green, green cotton jersey,
prince of the clean sheets—some upright insect
boxed between the sticks, the horizontal
and the pitch, stood with something up his sleeve,
armed with a pouch of tobacco and skins
to roll his own, or else a silver tin
containing eight or nine already rolled.
That's him with one behind his ear, between
his lips, or one tucked out of sight and lit—
a stamen cupped in the bud of his fist.
That's him sat down, not like those other clowns,
performing acrobatics on the bar, or press-ups
in the box, or running on the spot,
togged out in turtleneck pyjama-suits
with hands as stunted as a bunch of thumbs,
hands that are bandaged or swaddled with gloves,
laughable, frying-pan, sausage-man gloves.
Not my man, though, that's not what my man does;
a man who stubs his reefers on the post
and kicks his heels in the stud-marks and butts,
lighting the next from the last, in one breath
making the save of the year with his legs,
taking back a deep drag on the goal-line
in the next; on the one hand throwing out
or snaffling the ball from a high corner,
flicking off loose ash with the other. Or
in the freezing cold with both teams snorting
like flogged horses, with captains and coaches
effing and jeffing at backs and forwards,
talking steam, screaming exhausting orders,

that's not breath coming from my bloke, it's smoke.
Not him either goading the terraces,
baring his arse to the visitors' end
and dodging the sharpened ten-pence pieces,
playing up, picking a fight, but that's him
cadging a light from the ambulance men,
loosing off smoke rings, zeros or halos
that drift off, passively, over the goals
into nobody's face, up nobody's nose.
He is what he is, does whatever suits him,
because he has no highfalutin song
to sing, no neat message for the nation
on the theme of genius or dedication;
in his passport, under "occupation,"
no one forced the man to print the word
"custodian," and in *The Faber Book
of Handy Hints* his five-line entry reads:
"You young pretenders, keepers of the nought,
the nish, defenders of the sweet fuck-all,
think bigger than your pockets, profiles, health;
better by half to take a sideways view,
take a tip from me and deface yourselves."

A WEEK AND A FORTNIGHT

Tricked into life with a needle and knife
but marked with the cross in the eye of a rifle,
laid from the first in the grave of a cradle.

Fed with the flesh not the fur of a peach
but bruised in the garden, tripped in the street,
bunged with a bottle of petrol and bleach.

Nursed at the breast on the cream of the nipple
but branded for keeps with the print of a fist,
buffed with a handkerchief, flannelled with spittle.

Baubled and bangled from ankle to wrist
but milked for a season, stung by a cousin,
dunked for a bet on the hob of an oven.

Picked for a prize for the fair of his face
but kicked to the foot from the head of the stairs,
buckled and belted and leathered and laced.

Spared from a stunt in the mouth of a lion
but dabbed on the foot with a soldering iron,
stabbed in the palm with a smouldering stub.

Left for an hour with booze and a razor
but carted by ambulance clear of the woods,
saved at the last by drugs and a laser.

Days for the dirty, life for the lost,
the acts of mercy and the stations of the cross,
the seven acts of mercy and the fourteen stations of the cross.

DREAM HOLIDAY

On the first night, a yawn,
the noiseless opening and closing of a downstairs door.
The dog lifted an ear,
and the next day the dog was kennelled in the car.

On the next night, a sneeze or cough
was shredded paper or a flash-gun going off.
The dog tapped its tail,
and the next night the dog was taken out and docked.

On the third night, footsteps in the roof-space
were bars of gold loaded into a suitcase.
The dog yelped,
and there and then the dog was muzzled with a belt.

On the fourth night, the Milky Way
was the gang of sparks from a nylon stocking lifted
from a face; water in the cistern
whispered, the dog whimpered;

toenails clipped were cables snipped, cracked knuckles
were connections uncoupled; splintered wood
and fractured glass, the dog shat,
and for that the dog was taken out and shot.

On the last night we were cleaned out,
the sound of tearing metal—hinges, locks—
drowned by the thought
of a dog asleep like a stone in its box.

CHAPTER AND VERSE

They were ushered along to the water's edge
to wait. Then one further back on the bank
said drink, so they drank, some of them
cupping their hands, taking the water like gods,
and some of them kneeling and lapping the water
like dogs.

And those that had sunk to their knees, gone down
on all fours, they were taken aside and tried
for stooping as low as a beast, but moreover
for kissing themselves on the lips in the lake.
They were all of them guilty and gathered together
and thumped. In the face. And those that were saved
were rewarded with mirrors and cups and praise
having made at the lake such a lasting impression.

Here endeth the first lesson.

THE TWO OF US
(after Laycock)

You sat sitting in your country seat
with maidens, servants waiting hand and foot.
You eating swan, crustaceans, starters, seconds, sweet.
You dressed for dinner, worsted, made to measure. Cut:
me darning socks, me lodging at the gate,
me stewing turnips, beet, one spud,
a badger bone. Turf squealing in the grate—
no coal, no wood.

No good. You in your splendour: leather,
rhinestone, ermine, snakeskin, satin, silk,
a felt hat finished with a dodo feather.
Someone's seen you swimming lengths in gold-top milk.
Me parched, me in a donkey jacket,
brewing tea from sawdust mashed in cuckoo spit,
me waiting for the peaks to melt, the rain to racket
on the metal roof, the sky to split,

and you on-stream, piped-up, plugged-in, you worth a mint
and tighter than a turtle's snatch.
Me making light of making do with peat and flint
for heat, a glow-worm for a reading lamp. No match.
The valleys where the game is, where the maize is—
yours. I've got this plot just six foot long
by three foot wide, for greens for now, for daisies
when I'm dead and gone.

You've got the lot, the full set:
chopper, Roller, horse-drawn carriage, microlight, skidoo,
a rosewood yacht, a private jet.
I'm all for saying that you're fucking loaded, you.
And me, I clomp about on foot from field to street;
these clogs I'm shod with, held together now with segs
and fashioned for my father's father's father's feet—
they're on their last legs.

Some in the village reckon we're alike, akin:
same neck, same chin. Up close that's what they've found,
some sameness in the skin,
or else they've tapped me on the back and you've turned round.
Same seed, they say, same shoot,
like i'm some cutting taken from the tree,
like I'm some twig related to the root.
But I can't see it, me.

So when it comes to nailing down the lid
if I were you I wouldn't go with nothing.
Pick some goods and chattels, bits and bobs like Tutankhamen
        did,
and have them planted in the coffin.
Opera glasses, fob-watch, fountain pen, a case of fishing flies,
a silver name-tag necklace full-stopped with a precious stone,
a pair of one-pound coins to plug the eyes,
a credit card, a mobile phone,

some sentimental piece of earthenware,
a collar stud, a cufflink and a tiepin,
thirteen things to stand the wear and tear
of seasons underground, and I'll take what I'm standing up in.

That way, on the day they dig us out
they'll know that you were something really fucking fine
and I was nowt.
Keep that in mind,

because the worm won't know your make of bone from mine.

FIVE ELEVEN NINETY NINE

The makings of the fire to end all fires,
the takings of the year, all kinds of cane
and kindling to begin with, tinder sticks,
the trunk and branches of a silver birch

brought down by lightning, dragged here like a plough
through heavy earth from twenty fields away.
Timber: floorboards oiled and seasoned, planking,
purlins, sleepers, pelmets, casements, railings,

sacks of sweepings, splinters, sawdust, shavings.
Items on their own: a fold-away bed,
an eight-foot length of four-by-two, a pew,
a tea chest—empty, three piano legs,

a mantelpiece and a lazy Susan,
a table-top, the butt of a shotgun,
a toilet-seat, two-thirds of a triptych,
a Moses basket with bobbins in it,

a pair of ladders, half a stable-door,
a stump, one stilt, the best part of a boat,
a sight-screen stolen from the cricket field,
a hod, a garden bench, a wagon wheel.

We guess the place, divine it, dig a hole
then plant and hoist and pot the centre pole—
tall, redwood-size, of the telegraph type,
held tight with guy-ropes, hawsers, baling wire—

and for a week it has to stand alone,
stand for itself, a mark, a line of sight,
a stripe against the sky. Steeple, needle,
spindle casting half a mile of shadow

at dusk, at dawn another half-mile more.
Held down, held firm, but not to climb or scale;
strung, stayed, but with an element of play—
in wind the top nods inches either way.

Thing to surround, build around, or simply
the solid opposite of a chimney.
Symbol, signal, trigger for those people
who deliver all things combustible

this time of year, who rummage through attics
and huts, cellars and sheds, people who check
the yards and feet and inches of their lives
for something safe to sacrifice, figures

who visit the site, arrive with a box
and set it down like a child's coffin, or
those who come after dark, before first light,
with black bags that are bursting with something

and nothing. Rolls of oilcloth are carted
by hand. A furlong of carpet appears
that must have been brought here by van. Some kid
comes a mile and a third, uphill, to tip

a hundredweight of paper from a pram,
and a man turns up to empty a bin,

does so, picks through the garbage, finds a thing
or two—a ball of string, a leather shoe—

loads up and takes his findings home with him.
Later still that man comes back with a rough
half-full half-empty sack of low-grade coal—
offensive now within this smokeless zone—

and lugs it, wears it draped around his neck
like a dead foal, one hand hold of each end;
then on his knee he lays it down. Two coals
run out like two rats across the hard ground.

Such comings, givings, goings. Morning finds
the pole upstanding through a tractor tyre—
half a ton, those, so how did that get there?
All else scattered, as if dropped from the air,

litter brought from somewhere else to right here
by act of God or twister, washed ashore and beached
by long-shore drift and gale-force winds
and a hard night of high seas. Flotsam. Dreck.

We stack the fire at the eleventh hour,
begin by propping staves and leaning splints
against the centre-piece, build up and out
from slats and rafters through to joists and beams,

take notice of its changing shape: a cairn
becoming wigwam, then becoming dome,
becoming pyramid, then bell, then cone.
It has its features: priest holes, passageways,

a box-room, alcoves, doors. We hide and hoard,
stack bales of paper soused in paraffin
within its walls, stow blankets doused in oil,
load every seam with goods—goods to take hold—

and thread each flash point with a length of rope
soaked through with petrol, kerosene or meths
and trail the loose end to a distant place.
Unnecessary, but a nice touch, though.

That moment, then, before the burning starts—
like waiting for the tingle in the track
before the train, or on the empty road
before the motorcade, the time it takes

each elephant to wander from lightning
to thunder. That, or something in the bones
or in the weather, on the wind, a twinge
within the works of some barometer,

shouts of timber in the coral canyon
of the ear, the smell of burning pouring
through the chambers of the nose, a voltage
in the glades and groves of cells and glands. Hands

hang fire, hang loose in pairs of leather gloves,
and coolant flows and fills the trunks and roots
and limbs and leaves and needles of the lungs.
Then someone makes a move, a match gets struck . . .

The hiss first of damp wood, the fizz of steam,
a water-coloured flame, cradled and cupped

in a sheltered place, then circled and snuffed
by a twist of smoke. Something else flares up,

then chokes—a flame blown out by its own breath—
and a third and fourth are checked. More smoke
without fire, then a further space alive
with light, a chamber deep inside aglow

for good this time, fuelled with the right stuff,
feeding on something for just long enough
to tempt another thing to burn, combust,
to spread its word, to chatter its own name

through a stook of canes, to start a whisper
here and there that spreads across the broad base,
a rumour handed down, passed round and shared.
Heat dealt to every point, backed up by flames.

Sounds—the popping of corn, cars back-firing.
And sharps and flats, affricates, fricatives,
screams, an acetylene torch igniting,
a pilot light—its circular breathing.

The animal squeal of air escaping.
Snapping of soft wood—the bones of babies.
The depth-charge of a blown-out metal drum.
A pressurized can goes off like a gun,

at which a fox cuts loose from the fire, there
then gone, having waited this long to bolt
like a ball of light that breaks from the skin
of the sun; that explodes then dies. Like so,

observed through special telescopes, that is.
Lit from the front, the faces we wear
are masks, and bare hands hang down from their cuffs
like lamps. Heat to our hearts, but we each feel

the bite of frost from the nape of the neck
to the heels, a cold current through the spine
despite a hugging of duds: Russian dolls—
two shirts, three jumpers, jacket, anorak,

topped by an uncle's outsize overcoat.
A lending of heat and light to the air
but splinters of ice in our hands and hair.
Nothing to swing the weather vane, no breeze,

but down an avenue of silent trees
a dog walks a man through a rain of leaves.
Far detail: a goods-train hauling road-stone
wheel-spins at a set of signals. Diesel.

An hour later, though, the fire deep-seated,
up to speed, at full tilt. A garage roof,
bituminous, slides forward in the heat.
A window pops from its frame. A small girl

paddles in the puddle of her own boots,
melted to her feet. A man with an oar
comes forward from the crowd with a bauble
or a silver orb on its outstretched blade—

a cooking apple cased in baking foil—
which he expertly lays at the white heart

of the flames. "For eating, later," he says,
then stabs the fire and swipes the leading edge

of the burning oar no more than an inch
or so from the hat on the balding head
of his brother-in-law. Then shoulders it,
carries it like a banner, turns around,

and then ditches it, pitches it forward;
the sharp end finds the earth, digs in, goes out.
A grown man singes his eyebrows and screams.
And a wet dog sings in a cloud of steam.

A man who is blind walks down from his hill,
through the woods, having sensed a form of light
on his face when he raised his head, and heard
convected cinders raining on his roof.

A decent blaze, he says, but a shadow
of those in the past, of course, in the days
when smoke was mistaken for night, when fires
would singe an eyebrow from a mile away

or roast a chestnut hanging on its branch
or brown the skin through several layers of clothes.
One year his sister wore a floral blouse;
the next that she knew she was tanned with shapes

of bluets, goosefoot and morning glory.
Fires so full of the sun that each brought on
a second spring, an autumn flowering
of lilies, sesame and panic grass

and feverfew. And sickle senna too.
Another year a farmer drove a herd
of bullocks through the flames, and some came through
unscathed, but others fell, and ribs and steaks

were there to eat for those who wanted them.
But worst, the season he remembers most,
when seven children in a paper chase
holed up inside the mound of bric-a-brac

to be fired that night, and slept. And the rest
was a case of identification
by watches and lockets, fillings and teeth.
Someone gets the man a drink, and a seat.

And buildings swim in the haze of the heat.
And rockets set out for parks and gardens
and nose-dive into purple streets. And sparks
make the most of some moments of stardom.

And flakes of ash and motes of soot float up,
cool down, fall out, then go to ground. No sign,
no trace, unless they settle on the skin,
unless they come to hand or find a face

to brush or smudge or dust or break against.
And panes of glass take a shine to the fire,
and glass to all sides is amazed with light,
and every surface of a similar type

carries a torch, becomes inflamed. And eyes
if they blink are ablaze on the inside.

Gunpowder battles it out in the sky
where rockets go on unzipping the night.

Two or three at a time each firework blooms,
opens up fruits of sodium yellows
and calcium reds, shades of strontium
and copper—copper green and copper blue.

The tease of a paper fuse, then gunsmoke
shot with potash fumes, and cordite nosing
out of every empty barrel, casing,
tube. And several figures surround each squib,

and each and every huddle of people,
adults and kids, is the cast and crew
of its own short film, fifteen seconds long
at most and flickering—not black and white

but tinted in tones of alloys and chromes.
A soundtrack of sibilants, clacks and clicks,
and thuds and shrieks that are harder to place—
warfare or birdsong, peacocks or bombshells,

air raids, kittiwakes. And familiar sights,
like a Catherine wheel escaping its tail,
a Roman candle that snowballs the moon.
Clear skies, a night with its lid taken off

but peppered and strafed with fractals and flak,
gerbes and Saxons, star shells, Mines of Serpents,
Bengal Lights and other coruscations,
and the fire, glazing every act and scene

with versions of orange and tangerine,
the woods to the east thrown over with pink
and with crimson. There are cats in those woods,
they reckon, wild ones. Cats, and also mink,

but no one alive to swear they've seen them.
And a wheel of cheese—the moon on the rise,
caught like a ball in the branches of trees.
And a heat so solid now, a hard glow

we take for granted, easy come and go,
light years away from the era of flint
and stone and steel, the friction of dry sticks, the times
of trees ignited by bolts of lightning,

the untouchable gold of lava flow,
stories of sparks more precious than pearls
thrown up from the hooves of careering colts
or buffalo, struck from the beaks and claws

of eagles and hawks, and the days of flames
kept secret and safe in temples and caves.
Fire borrowed from neighbours and given back,
caught from the burning tail of a wild cat,

brought from the sun in the beak of a wren
or got from the glint in a precious gem.
Or fire snapped like twigs from red-berried trees,
bought from the otherworld, sought in the hearts

of warm-blooded things, under the stoat's tongue,
pulled from the nail of an old woman's thumb.

A distant cry from this surplus of heat,
as easily raised as falling asleep.

But then by one degree the brightness fades.
A fraction at first, it has to be said,
but then again the sun must pass its best
and move through noon the second that it strikes,

and in the space it takes to check a watch
another inch of time gets dropped, slides by,
is lost. The way it is with peaks and troughs—
that's how it goes with energy and clocks.

So we look to ourselves for something to burn,
to slow up the countdown of Centigrade,
but come up with metal: bedsteads and prams,
chains and a kettle, a bicycle frame.

A team of brothers walk further afield
to check the meadows of the north-north-east,
to comb the copse to the west of the creek,
to trawl for driftwood on the lakeside beach,

to haul the sunken jetty from the tarn,
then make a final circle of the town
and lift the stacks of litter from the streets.
They amble back with the following things:

a sack of potatoes going to seed,
a peacock feather, the skull of a sheep.
Thrown on, the feather shrinks then disappears,
the sack of spuds rolls over, waters, weeps;

with flames for eyes, the skull keeps its own shape.
Someone has to be to blame, so a man
who hasn't pulled his weight, who feeds his face
with coffee and cake is taken away.

Midnight is closing in. In steel-cap boots
and a boiler-suit, the friend of a friend
turns amber embers over with a spade,
splits wood in search of heat, looks for a pulse

within the charred remains of logs and stumps.
A girl who is said to be deaf and dumb
comes forward with a pitchfork and a brush
and turns and sweeps the margins of the flames

for seeds and knots and crumbs, chippings and thorns
that fizz and fry an inch above the heat,
then stops, then looks, then javels both the tools
into a fire that isn't hot enough

to detonate the bristles of the brush
or separate the two halves of the fork
by rapidly unseasoning the splice.
She backs off to a darker, silent place.

We stand in profile, figures from an age
before the dawn, paintings on a cave wall,
a people waiting for a word or sign,
one of the tribe to whisper something like

when one thing dies begin again inside;
look for it in the heartbeat of the tide,

wade in the coves and bays along the coast,
between the toes. Plot the zones and borders,

map the suburbs, boroughs, claim the polders,
sift the rapids five or six times over,
trace the water courses, mark the passes
and the gorges, plant and farm the ocean,

mow the steppes and fens and string the bridges
out between the contours of the ridges,
pick and pluck the cobweb of the matrix
of the districts, fly, align the air-strips,

take a section, make a transit, chart it,
pan the Gulf Stream, dive, way beneath the hull,
then rise towards the light until the head
comes up against the ice-cap of the skull . . .

But we have given all of what we own
and what we are, and it has come to this:
this spot, this date, this time, these tens of us,
all free but shadowless and primitive,

no more than silhouettes or negatives
or hieroglyphics, stark and shivering.
A half-life, heat-loss at a rate of knots,
an hour at most before the very last.

All lost. Until it dawns on one of us
to make the most of something from the past.
He walks us to a garage, picks the lock
and pinpoints with a torch a heavy cloth,

asbestos, woven, terrible to touch,
then covering his mouth against the dust
that blinks and glitters in the beam of light
he drags the cover from a wooden cross.

No time for measuring the shortest straw
or drawing lots. There's mention of a name,
and singled out the strongest of us bends
and takes its length along his spine, its frame

a crude flying machine, as someone says,
and takes its width across his arms and neck,
its point of balance bending him double
with dead weight as he walks, or rather wades.

And children point and poke fun at his shape,
this tottering man, like a living grave.
Even the dog at his side cocks a leg.
An aeroplane mimics him overhead.

We guide him to the left towards the site
through ginnels where his wing-span clips the sides
of houses, makes a xylophone of pipes
and railings, drum-rolls on a picket fence

and likewise once again along a length
of paling, then through parkland, puddles, sludge,
the tail-end ploughing, paying out a groove
between his footprints planted in the mud,

then onto concrete paving where he halts
above a hopscotch pattern sketched in chalk.

And there he falls, but stands up straight and walks
beneath a window where his mother waves

and calls his name, warns him to tie his boots
or lose his feet. He climbs a dozen steps,
then rests, by leaning with his arm outstretched,
hand flat against a wall. For a short while

we take the strain, but he loads up again
and makes for the faint light at the far end
of the lane, where a woman seems to wait
to produce a handkerchief trimmed with lace

from inside her sleeve, and to wipe his face.
He drops a second time and then a third,
but rounds the final corner on his knees
and kicks for home when he sees the remains

of the light and heat, and raises the cross
to its full height, and hugs it like a bear.
Upright, it seems to have doubled in size.
Whatever he wears is filthy and torn,

the pins and needles of splinters and spells
are under his nails and deep in his hands
like thorns. And when he tears himself away
it stays, held up by nothing more than air.

However, mass like that, the sort, weighed flat,
to break a back or trip a heart attack,
amounts to nothing stacked; and yet a hair
can trigger it, a tap from something slight

can topple it, say timber and it tips.
In this case someone serves up half a brick
that clips the crosspiece on the left-hand arm;
it twists, turns face about, tilts and quickens,

mimics the act of launching a discus,
the east and west of its cardinal points
beginning to roll, its axis falling
out of centre, out of true. Then it lands—

a noiseless splashdown in a pool of ash
invoking a mushroom of sparks and chaff
that takes its time to winnow and settle,
to clear. Hats in the air, and a loud cheer.

And it simmers and stews in its own steam,
then ignites. Those expecting an incense
of palm and cedar, the scent of olive
and cypress, are surprised by the odour

of willow and oak and pine and alder,
resins and oils from the Colne and Calder
that babble and lisp as they mix with fire.
Warmth for an hour, but not a minute more.

And blackness follows every burst of flames
that leaves us cold again, hands pocketed,
outdone, outshone, left in the shade by stars
that boil with light when the dark inflames them,

put to shame by shapes and constellations
that were dead and countersunk and buried,

hammered home in deep space. Like the new view
of the full moon, on full beam, in full bloom,

the open silver flower of the moon,
the boulder of the moon or the moon's shield,
hallmarked with valleys and rivers and fields,
the streams and snakes and fossils of the moon,

the long plumbago nights and graphite days,
the mercury seas and mercury lakes
of the moon, the moon on a plate, the date
and the name and the make of the full moon.

Under which we figure out the next move.
Off to the west, at the boarding kennels,
low down in the fringe of the sky, level
with chimneys, the crowns of trees and pylons,

a star, four-sided, breaks the horizon—
light in the shape of a dormer window—
and out of its frame a man emerges,
naked and bald and mad, head and shoulders,

and says his piece, shouts the odds about dogs
and vomit, fools returning to folly,
and the hounds in his keeping fratch and fret
or clatter the mesh of his twelve-foot fence.

And on the one hand someone rattles off
the preconditions, lists them one by one:
for little, wedding, middle, index, thumb,
read pressure, discharge, friction, action, heat

of any kind. But on the other hand
the things we're up against: clay, fibro, lime,
the silicates and tungstates, certain salts
and sodas, borax, alum; more than five,

not counting water and things of that kind.
Scissors cut paper and paper wraps rock,
rock blunts the scissors but water, water
swamps and dulls and rusts and dampens the lot.

Nothing else for it. The tightest of men
makes a move for his wallet, goes through it
for fivers, tenners and twenty-pound notes
and lets them drift to the little that's left

of the incandescence, like petals, picked
for the purpose of proving love, or not.
Another takes a last look through a deck
of snapshots, passport-size, in black and white,

then deals that pack of thirteen photographs
to the fire, the way some poker player
sits and tosses cards into a cocked hat.
And each image burns with a true colour.

Another burns a book of stamps, a cheque,
a calling-card, goes through his pockets, finds
and flings a ticket stub, a serviette,
a driving licence, birth certificate.

Another pulls a hip flask from his side,
empties it out on a mound of briquette;

the liquid vaporizes into scent:
angelica, wormwood, star-anise, mint.

He turns to us and tells us what it is
or what it was, and then pockets the flask.
Another strips his friend of his flat cap,
prizes it from him like a bottle top,

then slings it, frisbee-style, into the ash.
Another man decapitates himself
or so it looks from here, beheads himself
it seems, unzips the detachable hood

from his coat for the sake of the lost cause,
looks for a naked flame, and on it goes.
And on it goes: a pair of gloves, a scarf,
a balaclava lifted from a face.

The act of keeping warm by burning clothes—
like eating your own hand to stay alive
or tapping your arm for a quart of blood
to survive. Tell that to the starving, though,

and the dry, those of us feeling the cold
tonight. We follow suit, burn every stitch
for one last wave of heat, pixel of light.
Unbuttoned but thankfully out of sight

except in the eye of the moon, silent
except for the padding of feet, bare feet,
we turn to go, then go together, home
in numbers, then in pairs and then alone

to houses ransacked and reduced to stone,
uncurtained windows, doors without doors,
to rooms that are skeletal, stripped, unmade,
to beds without cover, lamps without shade.

At dawn, through living daylight, half asleep,
we drift back to the place, which brings to mind
a crater punched home by a meteorite
or else a launch-pad or a testing-site.

Kicking through the feather-bed of ashes
someone flushes out a half-baked apple.
Softened, burnt and blistered on the skin, but
hardly touched within. Inedible thing,

the flesh gone muddy, foul, the core and pips
that no one cares to eat still fresh, still ripe,
and him who found it heads off down the slope
towards the park and plants or buries it.

We wait, listless, aimless now it's over,
ready for what follows, what comes after,
stood beneath an iron sky together,
awkwardly at first, until whenever.

ROBINSON'S LIFE SENTENCE

Rise early from a double bed,
take a shower, tie off the blind,
another dawn like open-heart surgery,
mosey downstairs, brew up, take time
over the papers, the results,
the notices, zip up, step out, bookworm
and browse down the high street,
pay for something by cheque or plastic,
see a man unhitch a sidecar
from his silver motorcycle, then
leave it there like a baby's shoe,
meet a friend, make a new friend,
take a drink, eat, talk shop,
re-string the steel guitar, scratch out
a new tune, try out someone's car for size,
buy oil or petrol by cheque or plastic,
make that call, write that card,
send out for supper, get stewed
on straight gin, turn in,
read a little, backpedal
through some old editions, crash out
and sleep like a bear, washed by wave
after wave of gentle dreams, but
wake again, and rise early.

SONG OF THE WEST MEN

To the far of the far
off the isles of the isles,
near the rocks of the rocks
which the guillemots stripe
with the shite of their shite,

a trawler went down
in the weave of the waves,
and a fisherman swam
for the life of his life
through the swell of the sea

which was one degree C.
And the bones of his bones
were cooler than stone,
and the tide of his blood
was slower than slow.

He met with the land
where the cliffs of the cliffs
were steeper than sheer,
where the sheep had to graze
by the teeth of their teeth.

So he put out again
for the beach,
and made it to lava
that took back his skin
to the feet of his feet,

and arrived at a door
with a tenth of a tale
that was taller than tall,
as cold and as bled as a man
from a fridge. But he lived.

The good of the good
will come this way, they say:
tattered and torn,
unlikely and out of the storm
if it comes at all.

TACHOGRAPH

West, alongside running water, low gear climbing cinder tracks, around elbow-angles, dropping it down for the revs, driving the bends, taking the view from a passing-place. Over the brow of the first in the range, spot-height to the east, checked and named, through a cutting or pass, eyes to the front, four miles one-in-five downhill, test the brakes. West, sweet-going single track beside a silver-plated lake, metalled at last, slow up for the bridges, narrow gauge, breathe in, nearside and offside mirrors for whiskers, spare inches. West, fallen boulders, road closed unpassable out of season, five ptarmigan up ahead like tea cosies, hikers, ten miles to travel one, fjords—up to the armpit and out to the fingertip of each, back onto grit, window up, this year's gravel sluiced by rain, pot-holes and pits, bedrock jiggered by frost, hard on the hands on the wheel, hard on the seat. West, half a junction coming up, good use of the map, good trig, incline to highest point, tightrope between two peaks, arête, pig-iron fence, head in the clouds, sweep down into arable land, common fields, fair going over level ground, front-wheel-drive with back end sliding around, shell out for diesel, last chance before Newfoundland. Still west along contour, following earthflow, downthrow, hanging valleys unjugging milk-like melt-water, into neutral with the slope, radio search for World Service, crank up the tape, foothills ahead, kettle-holes up to the hubs, survival shelter high to the left, new view, cover crops holding acres in place, the freight of ourselves carried in oo—scale over epic terrain, floodplain, bays and bights, essential minerals close at hand, noble metals, mantle on top, up and over banks of kame, intermittent rain, hardpan over there swept clean for the landing of planes, square miles of acid rock, homesteads under the bluff, last farm, last

light before west, land-breeze picking up, relief, horizon at last
of sea unbroken, ledge-road under the cliffs, headlights on dip,
blue-vein lode in the stones, sunstruck at the coast, free-wheel
down out of landscape numb with after-shock, end of the day,
handbrake stop.

A GLORY

Right here you made an angel of yourself,
free-falling backwards into last night's snow,
indenting a straight, neat, crucified shape,
then flapping your arms, one stroke, a great bird,
to leave the impression of wings. It worked.
Then you found your feet, sprang clear of the print
and the angel remained, fixed, countersunk,
open wide, hosting the whole of the sky.

Losing sleep because of it, I backtrack
to the place, out of earshot of the streets,
above the fetch and reach of the town.
The scene of the crime. Five-eighths of the moon.
On ground where snow has given up the ghost
it lies on its own, spread-eagled, embossed,
commending itself, star of its own cause.
Priceless thing—the faceless hood of the head,
grass making out through the scored spine, the wings
on the turn, becoming feathered, clipped.

Cattle would trample roughshod over it,
hikers might come with pebbles for the eyes,
a choice of fruit for the nose and the lips;
somebody's boy might try it on for size,
might lie down in its shroud, might suit, might fit. Angel,
from under the shade and shelter of trees
I keep watch, wait for the dawn to take you,
raise you, imperceptibly, by degrees.

THE TYRE

Just how it came to rest where it rested,
miles out, miles from the last farmhouse even,
was a fair question. Dropped by hurricane
or aeroplane perhaps for some reason,
put down as a cairn or marker, then lost.
Tractor-size, six or seven feet across,
it was sloughed, unconscious, warm to the touch,
its gashed, rhinoceros, sea-lion skin
nursing a gallon of rain in its gut.
Lashed to the planet with grasses and roots,
it had to be cut. Stood up it was drunk
or slugged, wanted nothing more than to slump,
to spiral back to its circle of sleep,
dream another year in its nest of peat.
We bullied it over the moor, drove it,
pushed from the back or turned it from the side,
unspooling a thread in the shape and form
of its tread, in its length and in its line,
rolled its weight through broken walls, felt the shock
when it met with stones, guided its sleepwalk
down to meadows, fields, onto level ground.
There and then we were one connected thing,
five of us, all hands steering a tall ship
or one hand fingering a coin or ring.

Once on the road it picked up pace, free-wheeled,
then moved up through the gears, and wouldn't give
to shoulder-charges, kicks; resisted force
until to tangle with it would have been
to test bone against engine or machine,

to be dragged in, broken, thrown out again
minus a limb. So we let the thing go,
leaning into the bends and corners,
balanced and centred, riding the camber,
carried away with its own momentum.
We pictured an incident up ahead:
life carved open, gardens in half, parted,
a man on a motorbike taken down,
a phone-box upended, children erased,
police and an ambulance in attendance,
scuff-marks and the smell of burning rubber,
the tyre itself embedded in a house
or lying in the gutter, playing dead.
But down in the village the tyre was gone,
and not just gone but unseen and unheard of,
not curled like a cat in the graveyard, not
cornered in the playground like a reptile,
or found and kept like a giant fossil.
Not there or anywhere. No trace. Thin air.

Being more in tune with the feel of things
than science and facts, we knew that the tyre
had travelled too fast for its size and mass,
and broken through some barrier of speed,
outrun the act of being driven, steered,
and at that moment gone beyond itself
towards some other sphere, and disappeared.

THE WINNER

When the feeling went in the lower half of my right arm
they fitted a power-tool into the elbow joint
with adjustable heads. When I lost the left
they gave me a ball on a length of skipping-rope
and I played the part of a swingball post
on a summer lawn for a circle of friends.
After the pins and needles in my right leg
they grafted a shooting stick onto the stump.
When septicaemia took the other peg
I thanked the mysterious ways of the Lord
for the gift of sight and my vocal cords.
With the brush in my teeth, I painted Christmas cards.
When I went blind, they threaded light-bulbs
into the sockets, and slotted a mouth-organ
into the groove of the throat when cancer struck.
For ears, they kitted me out with a baby's sock
for one, and a turned-out pocket, sellotaped on.

Last autumn I managed the Lyke Wake Walk,
forty-odd miles in twenty-four hours—oh Ma,
treasure this badge that belongs to your son
with his nerves of steel and his iron will.
This Easter I'm taking the Life-saving Test—oh Pa,
twenty-five lengths of the baths towing a dead weight,
picture your son in his goggles and vest, with a heart
like a water-pump under a battleship chest.

FOR THE RECORD

Ever since the very brutal extraction
of all four of my wisdom teeth,
I've found myself talking
with another man's mouth, so to speak,
and my tongue has become a mollusc
such as an oyster or clam,
broken and entered, licking
its wounds in its shell.

I was tricked into sleep by a man with a smile,
who slipped me the dose
like a great-uncle slipping his favourite nephew
a ten-pound note, like
so, back-handed, then tipped me a wink.
I was out with the stars,
and woke up later, crying,
and wanting to hold the hand of the nurse.

Prior to that, my only experience
under the knife was when I was five,
when my tonsils were hanging
like two bats at the back of a cave
and had to be snipped. But that
was a piece of piss compared with this,
which involved, amongst other things,
three grown men, a monkey-wrench

and the dislocation of my jaw. I wonder,
is this a case of excessive force,

like the powers-that-be evicting
a family of four, dragging them
kicking and screaming, clinging to furniture,
out through their own front door?
Like drawing all four corners of the earth
through the Arc de Triomphe.

You might think that with all the advances
in medical science
teeth like these could be taken out
through the ears or the anus,
or be shattered like kidney stones
by lasers from a safe distance.
But it seems that the art
hasn't staggered too far since the days

when a dentist might set up his stall
at a country fair
or travelling circus.
I'm also reminded of John Henry Small
of Devizes, who put his fist in his mouth
but couldn't spit it out,
and the hand was removed, forthwith,
along with his canines and incisors.

Returning to myself, the consultant says
I should wait another week at least
before saying something in haste
which at leisure I might come to repent.
But my mouth still feels

like a car with its wheels stolen, propped up
on bricks, and I'm unhappy about the way
they stitched the tip of my tongue

to my cheek.

HOMECOMING

Think, two things on their own and both at once.
The first, that exercise in trust, where those in front
stand with their arms spread wide and free-fall
backwards, blind, and those behind take all the weight.

The second, one canary-yellow cotton jacket
on a cloakroom floor, uncoupled from its hook,
becoming scuffed and blackened underfoot. Back home
the very model of a model of a mother, yours, puts
two and two together, makes a proper fist of it
and points the finger. Temper, temper. Questions
in the house. You seeing red. Blue murder. Bed.

Then midnight when you slip the latch and sneak
no further than the call-box at the corner of the street;
I'm waiting by the phone, although it doesn't ring
because it's sixteen years or so before we'll meet.
Retrace that walk towards the garden gate; in silhouette
a father figure waits there, wants to set things straight.

These ribs are pleats or seams. These arms are sleeves.
These fingertips are buttons, or these hands can fold
into a clasp, or else these fingers make a zip
or buckle, you say which. Step backwards into it
and try the same canary-yellow cotton jacket, there,
like this, for size again. It still fits.

8 P.M. AND RAINING WHEN ROBINSON

arrives by bus in a town whose name
he would not care to mention,
sets his baggage down,
hails a taxi and pays a fiver, his heart
in his mouth, Robinson
saying, "There's a road goes east, take it

for one mile then drop me. If there's change, you keep it."
No names,
then, "Hey, you're Robinson,
I saw that piece in the *Racing Post* . . ." One mention
of himself and Robinson's heart
takes off with itself like a horse in a hailstorm, down

to the car park under the covered market, down
to that glove compartment where he left it . . .
empty! Robinson's heart
sinks like an anchor. Mud now, his name,
and only minutes till they find him and mention
the million dollar question. "Robinson,"

his doctor once told him, "Robinson,
you should take things steady, son. Calm down."
But his nerves, his hair, not to mention
his face looking more each day like a Photofit.
In heaven's name
they should finish him off but they haven't a heart

between them. Sprinting now, each beat of his heart
gazumping the next—take that, Robinson.

Someone drops his name
in a doorway, a body check brings him down,
they hold out his tongue and lean a blade against it:
"Next time you squeak, Robinson, one more mention

and you're sausage meat. Mention
us again and we'll twist out your heart
and you'll eat it,
we'll have your balls for a bow tie, Robinson,
you can write that down
if you need to, but breathe our name . . ."

Don't mention the plan: new town, new name,
two fingers to those heartless bastards, and settle down.
There's a bus in the station. Go for it, Robinson.

YOU'RE BEAUTIFUL

because you're classically trained.
I'm ugly because I associate piano wire with strangulation.

You're beautiful because you stop to read the cards in
        newsagents' windows
about lost cats and missing dogs.
I'm ugly because of what I did to that jellyfish with a lolly
        stick and a big stone.

You're beautiful because for you, politeness is instinctive, not
        a marketing campaign.
I'm ugly because desperation is impossible to hide.

> *Ugly like he is,*
> *Beautiful like hers,*
> *Beautiful like Venus,*
> *Ugly like his,*
> *Beautiful like she is,*
> *Ugly like Mars.*

You're beautiful because you believe in coincidence and the
        power of thought.
I'm ugly because I proved God to be a mathematical
        improbability.

You're beautiful because you prefer home-made soup to the
        packet stuff.
I'm ugly because once, at a dinner party,
I defended the aristocracy and wasn't even drunk.

You're beautiful because you can't work the remote control.
I'm ugly because of satellite television and twenty-four-hour
    rolling news.

> *Ugly like he is,*
> *Beautiful like hers,*
> *Beautiful like Venus,*
> *Ugly like his,*
> *Beautiful like she is,*
> *Ugly like Mars.*

You're beautiful because you cry at weddings as well as
    funerals.
I'm ugly because I think of children as another species from a
    different world.

You're beautiful because you look great in any colour
    including red.
I'm ugly because I think shopping is strictly for the
    acquisition of material goods.

You're beautiful because when you were born, undiscovered
    planets
lined up to peep over the rim of your cradle and lay gifts of
    gravity and light
at your miniature feet.
I'm ugly for saying "love at first sight" is another form of
    mistaken identity,
and that the most human of all responses is to gloat.

> *Ugly like he is,*
> *Beautiful like hers,*
> *Beautiful like Venus,*

Ugly like his,
Beautiful like she is,
Ugly like Mars.

You're beautiful because you've never seen the inside of a
    car-wash.
I'm ugly because I always ask for a receipt.

You're beautiful for sending a box of old shoes to the third
    world.
I'm ugly because I remember the telephone numbers of ex-
    girlfriends
and the year Schubert was born.

You're beautiful because you sponsored a parrot in the zoo.
I'm ugly because when I sigh it's like the slow collapse of a
    circus tent.

Ugly like he is,
Beautiful like hers,
Beautiful like Venus,
Ugly like his,
Beautiful like she is,
Ugly like Mars.

You're beautiful because you can point at a man in a uniform
    and laugh.
I'm ugly because I was a police informer in a previous life.

You're beautiful because you drink a litre of water and eat
    three pieces of fruit a day.
I'm ugly for taking the line that a meal without meat is a
    beautiful woman with one eye.

You're beautiful because you don't see love as a competition
and you know how to lose.
I'm ugly because I kissed the FA Cup then held it up to the
crowd.

You're beautiful because of a single buttercup in the top
buttonhole of your cardigan.
I'm ugly because I said the World's Strongest Woman was a
muscleman in a dress.

You're beautiful because you couldn't live in a lighthouse.
I'm ugly for making hand-shadows in front of the giant bulb,
so when they look up,
the captains of vessels in distress see the ears of a rabbit, or
the eye of a fox,
or the legs of a galloping black horse.

> *Ugly like he is,*
> *Beautiful like hers,*
> *Beautiful like Venus,*
> *Ugly like his,*
> *Beautiful like she is,*
> *Ugly like Mars.*

> *Ugly like he is,*
> *Beautiful like hers,*
> *Beautiful like Venus,*
> *Ugly like his,*
> *Beautiful like she is,*
> *Ugly like Mars.*

ALL FOR ONE

Why is it my mind won't leave me alone?
All day it sits on the arm of the chair
plucking grey hairs like thoughts out of my skull,
flicking my ear with a Duralon comb.

Evenings when I need to work, get things done;
nine o'clock, my mind stands with its coat on
in the hall. Sod it. We drive to the pub,
it drinks, so yours truly has to drive home.

I leave at sunrise in the four-wheel-drive—
my mind rides shotgun on the running board,
taps on the window of my log-cabin,
wants to find people and go night-clubbing.

Social call—my mind has to tag along.
Hangs off at first, plays it cool, smiles its smile;
next minute—launches into song. Then what?
Only cops off with the belle of the belle

of the ball—that's all. Main man. Life and soul.
Makes hand-shadows on the living-room wall.
Recites *Albert and the Lion,* in French,
stood on its head drinking a yard of ale.

Next morning over paracetamol and toast
my mind weeps crocodile tears of remorse
onto the tablecloth. *Can't we be close?*
I look my mind square in the face and scream:

mind, find your own family and friends to love;
mind, open your own high-interest account;
offer yourself the exploding cigar;
put whoopee-cushions under your own arse.

It's a joke. I flounce out through the front door;
my mind in its slippers and dressing gown
runs to the garden and catches my sleeve,
says what it's said a hundred times before.

From a distance it must look a strange sight:
two men of identical shape, at odds
at first, then joined by an outstretched arm, one
leading the other back to his own home.

CHAINSAW VERSUS THE PAMPAS GRASS

It seemed an unlikely match. All winter unplugged,
grinding its teeth in a plastic sleeve, the chainsaw swung
nose-down from a hook in the darkroom
under the hatch in the floor. When offered the can
it knocked back a quarter-pint of engine oil
and juices ran from its joints and threads,
oozed across the guide-bar and the maker's name,
into the dry links.

From the summerhouse, still holding one last gulp
of last year's heat behind its double doors, and hung
with the weightless wreckage of wasps and flies,
moth-balled in spider's wool . . .
from there, I trailed the day-glo orange power-line
the length of the lawn and the garden path,
fed it out like powder from a keg, then walked
back to the socket and flicked the switch, then walked again
and coupled the saw to the flex—clipped them together.
Then dropped the safety catch and gunned the trigger.

No gearing up or getting to speed, just an instant rage,
the rush of metal lashing out at air, connected to the main.
The chainsaw with its perfect disregard, its mood
to tangle with cloth, or jewellery, or hair.
The chainsaw with its bloody desire, its sweet tooth
for the flesh of the face and the bones underneath,
its grand plan to kick back against nail or knot
and rear up into the brain.
I let it flare, lifted it into the sun

and felt the hundred beats per second drumming in its heart,
and felt the drive-wheel gargle in its throat.

The pampas grass with its ludicrous feathers
and plumes. The pampas grass, taking the warmth and light
from cuttings and bulbs, sunning itself,
stealing the show with its footstools, cushions and tufts
and its twelve-foot spears.
This was the sledgehammer taken to crack the nut.
Probably all that was needed here was a good pull or shove
or a pitchfork to lever it out at its base.
Overkill. I touched the blur of the blade
against the nearmost tip of a reed—it didn't exist.
I dabbed at a stalk that swooned, docked a couple of heads,
dismissed the top third of its canes with a sideways sweep
at shoulder height—this was a game.
I lifted the fringe of undergrowth, carved at the trunk—
plant-juice spat from the pipes and tubes
and dust flew out as I ripped into pockets of dark, secret
        warmth.

To clear a space to work
I raked whatever was severed or felled or torn
towards the dead zone under the outhouse wall, to be fired.
Then cut and raked, cut and raked, till what was left
was a flat stump the size of a manhole cover or barrel lid
that wouldn't be dug with a spade or prized from the earth.
Wanting to finish things off I took up the saw
and drove it vertically downwards into the upper roots,
but the blade became choked with soil or fouled with weeds,
or what was sliced or split somehow closed and mended behind,
like cutting at water or air with a knife.
I poured barbecue fluid into the patch

and threw in a match—it flamed for a minute, smoked
for a minute more, and went out. I left it at that.

In the weeks that came new shoots like asparagus tips
sprang up from its nest and by June
it was riding high in its saddle, wearing a new crown.
Corn in Egypt. I looked on
from the upstairs window like the midday moon.

Back below stairs on its hook, the chainsaw seethed.
I left it a year, to work back through its man-made dreams,
to try to forget.
The seamless urge to persist was as far as it got.

THE STRID

After tying the knot,
whatever possessed us to make for the Strid?

That crossing point
on the River Wharfe

which famously did
for the boy and his dog;

that tourist trap
where a catchment area comes to a head

in a bottleneck stream
above Bolton Abbey;

you in your dress of double cream,
me done up like a tailor's dummy.

Surely it's more of a lover's leap:
two back-to-back rocks

hydraulically split
by the incompressible sap of the spine;

let it be known
that between two bodies made one

there's more going on
than they'd have us believe.

Whatever possessed us, though?
Was it the pink champagne talking?

Or all for the sake of carrying on,
canoodling out of doors,

the fuck of the century under the stars?
Or the leather-soled shoes

with the man-made uppers,
bought on the never-never,

moulded and stitched
for the purpose of taking us

up and across, over the threshold
of water-cut rock and localised moss

in one giant stride,
bridegroom and bride?

A week goes by,
then the rain delivers:

you, like the death of a swan
in a bed of reeds,

me, like a fish gone wrong
a mile down river;

exhibits X and Y,
matching rings on swollen fingers,

and proof beyond doubt
of married life—

the coroner's voice, proclaiming us
dead to the world, husband and wife.

THE TWANG

Well it was St. George's Day in New York.
They'd dyed the Hudson with cochineal and chalk.
Bulldogs were arse-to-mouth in Central Park.
Midtown, balloons drifted up, red and white streamers

flowed like plasma and milk. The Mayor on a float on Fifth,
resplendent, sunlight detonating on his pearly suit.
The President followed, doing the Lambeth Walk.
It was an election year on both counts. In the Royal Oak

boiled beef was going for a song. Some Dubliner
played along, came out with cockney rhyming-slang,
told jokes against his own and spoke of cousins twice removed
from Islington, which made him one of us.

A paper dragon tripped down Lexington, its tongue
truly forked. Two hands thrust from its open throat:
in the left, a red rose; in the right, a collection box
for the National Trust. I mean the National Front.

THE STRAND

We were two-and-a-half thousand miles west
and still putting miles on the clock, driving
at night, the small wooden towns of the coast
coming up in the rain like cargo adrift
then falling away into dark. The road
followed the swell of the land, riding the waves,
then slowed in a town whose name I forget,
a place picked with a pin and an old map
by pricking the bent finger of Cape Cod.
This time we meant it. This time we'd drawn blood.

Evening darkness. Trespass. Walking blindfold
down a private road to a public beach
to fuck, like an order, lie down and fuck.
If the lighthouse shoots us one of its looks,

so what. Then back to the Anglified room
with its Lloyd-loom chairs, its iron bedstead
like the gasworks gates, its Armitage Shanks,
electric candles and motorised drapes.
We dug out the cork from a bottle of red
with the car key, drank from the neck, then slept
naked and drunk on the four-poster bed
with its woolsack mattress and stage-coach springs.
The fire—a paper-pulp, look-alike log
in its own, flammable, touchpaper bag—
burnt down as neatly in the polished grate
as it should, made flames without smoke or ash

or heat, and got us to dream the endings
of afternoon films and old, hardback books.
A place like this could go up in a flash.

By day we looked for our octopus print
on the beach, but a high tide had been in
to clean and tidy the bay, to flush out
creases and seams. Houses of wood on stilts,
blasted by years and the flacking of salt,
stood back from the front, held on by their roots.
Rock pools were bleary with seaweed and brine.
We were writing our full names on the beach
with our bare feet when I stood on the bird.
Peeled from the sand, hauled and held by its bill,
its parasol wings swung open and out
in a sprained, unmendable twirl. Stone dead—
the sodden quills, the nerveless, leaden flesh.

This was the turning post, the furthest point.
Here was the archaeopteryx of guilt,
this dinosaur hatched from its fossil shell
to doodle-bug out of Atlantic skies
or strike home riding the push of the tide.
It had to be photographed, weighed and sized,
named and sexed, had to be hoisted and hung
by its sharp, arrowhead skull—like a kill.

Then what? Either I raised it to heaven,
arranged its bones as a constellation,
kept on running under the empty stars
of its eyes, under a snow of feathers.

Or I followed the fixed look on your face
to an unmarked circle of sand from where
we could double back, leave this gannet's corpse
beached between open water and blue sky,
eating into the beach, feeding the sea.

SALVADOR

He has come this far for the English to see,
arrived by bubble through a twelve-hour dream
of altitude sickness and relative speed, of leg room
and feet, headphone headache, reclining sleep.
Jet-lag slung from the eyes like hammocks at full stretch,
mefloquine pellets riding shotgun in a blister-pack.
This far south for the English to see, as they say.
The hotel drives towards him up the street,
he turns the keyhole anti-clockwise with the key,
the water spins the plug-hole backwards as it drains.
He counts the track-marks in his upper arm
and those in the buttocks and those in the calves,
the pins and needles of shots and jabs, strains and strands,
spores going wild in the tunnels and tubes of veins,
mushrooming into the brain. A polio spider
abseils the drop from the sink to the bath.
Lariam country—this far south to broaden the mind.
Look, learn, rise to the day, throw back the blind:
the blue-green flowers of the meningitis tree,
the two-note singing of the hepatitis bird,
the two-stroke buzz of the tetanus bee.
In a puff of chalk a yellow-fever moth
collides and detonates against the window frame.
Malaria witters and whines in the radio waves.
A warm, diphtherial breeze unsettles the pool.
Three hours behind and two days' growth—
hey you in the mirror, shaving in soap,
brushing your teeth in duty-free rum and mini-bar coke,
you with the look, you with the face—it's me, wake up.

THE GOLDEN TODDY

We hunted, swept the planet pole to pole
to capture a glimpse of that rare species.

Through a thermal lens we spotted the shoal,
picked up the trail of nuggety faeces

then tagged the shiniest beast in the pride,
mounted a camera on its gleaming horn,
bolted a microphone into its hide.
A first: toddies aflight, asleep, in spawn . . .

After months in the field, the broken yolks
had gilded and glazed the presenter's boots;
the sponsor's lover wore a precious skull
for a brooch, out-glinting the best boy's tooth.

Rank bad form. But the creature itself shone,
perched on the clapper-board, the golden one.

BIRTHDAY

Bed. Sheets without sleep, and the first birds.
Dawn at the pace of a yacht.

The first bus, empty, carries its cargo of light
from the depot, like a block of ice.

Dawn when the mind looks out of its nest,
dawn with gold in its teeth.

In the street, a milk-float moves
by throw of the dice,

the mast to the east raises itself
to its full height. Elsewhere

someone's husband touches someone's wife.
One day older the planet weeps.

This is the room
where I found you one night,

bent double, poring over
The Universal Home Doctor,

that bible of death, atlas of ill-health:
hand-drawn, colour-coded diagrams of pain,

chromosomal abnormalities explained,
progesterone secretion,

cervical incompetence . . .
Susan, for God's sake.

I had to edge towards it,
close the cover with my bare foot.

Dawn when the mind looks out of its nest.
Dawn with gold in its teeth.

From the window I watch
Anubis, upright in black gloves

making a sweep of the earth
under the nameless tree,

pushing through shrubs,
checking the bin for bones or meat

then leaving with a backward glance, in his own time,
crossing the lawn and closing the gate.

THE NIGHT-WATCHMAN

Waking in cold sweat, he thought of the miller
dunking his head in his day's work
to guard against theft from his precious flour,
sealing every grain and ground in place
with the look in his eye and the twist of his mouth.

Even a finger, licked and dabbed for a taste
would leave a print, a trace. Then thought

of the deep-sea diver or astronaut, home at last,
who peeled the bedspread from his bed and caught
a strange impression in the cotton sheet,
a new expression buried in the pillow-case
beside his wife, and stood

a lifelong minute on the ocean-floor of outer space,
lead-limbed, ashen-faced.

THE JAY

I was pegging out your lime-green dress;
you were hoping the last of the sun
might sip the last few beads of drip-dry water
from its lime-green hem.

I had a blister-stigmata the size of an eye
in the palm of my hand
from twisting the point of a screw
into the meat of the house. Those days. Those times.

The baby bird was crossing the gravel path
in the style of a rowing boat crossing dry land.
Struck with terror when I held it tight
in the gardening gloves of humankind, we saw for ourselves

the mouse-fur face and black moustache,
the squab of breast-meat under its throat,
the buff-brown coat and blue lapels,
the painted inside of its mouth,

the raw, umbilical flute of its tongue
sucking hard at the sky for a taste of air.
Setting it free, it managed no more than a butterfly stroke
to the shade of an evergreen tree, where we let it be.

They say now that the basis of life
in the form of essential carbon deposits
could have fallen to earth as a meteorite, or comet,
and that lightning strikes from banks of static

delivered the spark that set life spinning.
But this three-letter bird was death, death thrown in from above,
death as a crash-brained, bone-smashed, cross-feathered bullet,
so we could neither kill it nor love it.

THE SUMMERHOUSE

With the right tools it was less than a day's work.
It wasn't our trade, but a wire-brush was the thing
for fettling mould and moss from bevelled window frames.
Sandpaper took back old wood to its true grain.

Winter pressed its handshake, even through thick gloves.
From the boozy warmth of the boiler-room I lugged
a litre tin of Weatherseal, and popped the lid.
Strange brew. Varnish or paint? Water-based, it had a tone

or shade, but carried solvent on its breath
and held the stars and planets of a pinhole universe
suspended in its depth. Some gemstone in its liquid state—
it fumed when ruffled with a garden cane.

Winter stood on the toe-end of leather boots.
And as the substance in the tin went down it lost its shine,
and from its lower reaches came a sluggishness—
a thick, begrudging treacle, and the colour brown.

Some change in temperature was the root cause.
Rifles stamped their feet and clapped their hands together
over on the firing-range. It was going dark
but unconcerned we dipped the brushes for a second coat.

It was time-travel, of a sort. Having given our all
to this chapel of sun-loungers and soft drinks,
to the obvious glory of ultraviolet light, we found ourselves
standing instead by a wooden shed, painted with mud and shit.

THE ENGLISH

They are a gentleman farmer, living
on reduced means, a cricketer's widow
sowing a kitchen garden with sweet peas.
A lighthouse-keeper counting aeroplanes.

Old blackout curtains staunch the break of day.
Regard the way they dwell, the harking back:
how the women at home went soldiering on
with pillows for husbands, fingers for sons,

how man after man emerged at dawn
from his house, in his socks, then laced his boots
on the step, locked up, then steadied himself
to post a key back through the letterbox.

The afternoon naps, the quaint hours they keep.
But since you ask them, that is how they sleep.

WORKING FROM HOME

When the tree-cutter came with his pint-size mate,
I sat in the house but couldn't think.
For an hour he lurked in the undergrowth,
trimming the lower limbs, exposing the trunks.

I moved upstairs but there he was, countersunk eyes
and as bald as a spoon, emergent in orange rays,
head popping out through leafage or fir,
a fairy light in the tree of heaven,

a marker-buoy in the new plantation of silver pine.
Or traversing, bough to bough, from one dead elm
to the next, or holding on by his legs only,
or acrobranching the canopy. At lunch,

he pulled the wooden ladder up behind,
perched in the crown of a laurel, and smoked.
He nursed the petrol-driven chainsaw like a false arm.
The dwarf swept berries and beech-nuts into a cloth bag.

I was dodging between rooms now, hiding from view.
Down below they cranked up the chipping machine,
fed timber and brushwood into the hopper.
Through a gap in the curtains I looked, saw into its maw—

steel teeth crunching fishbone twigs,
chomping thick wood, gagging on lumber and stumps.
Sawdust rained into the caged truck.
Birds were flying into the arms of a scarecrow

on Pole Moor, or leaving for Spain. I sat on the steps
between ground-floor and upstairs, thought of his face
at the bathroom window watching me shave,
his lips in the letterbox, wanting to speak.

THE BACK MAN

Five strong, we were, not including the guide,
five of us walking a well-trodden path
through the reserve, from the camp to the stream
and the flooded forest on the far side.
Dragonflies motored past like fish on the wing.
Beetles lifted their solar-panelled shells.
A bird, invisible, ran through its scale
like a thumbnail strummed on a metal comb.
The branches of trees were shelves in a shop
selling insect brooches and snakeskin belts
and miniature frogs with enamelled heads.
The monkeys fancied themselves as soft toys.
Blue orchids offered themselves without shame.
Late afternoon, and the heat in the shade
was stale and gross, a queasy, airless warmth,
centuries old. I was the last in line,

the back man, when from out of nowhere
it broke, I mean flew at me from behind
and I saw in my mind's eye the carved mask
of its face, the famous robe of black fur,
the pins and amulets of claws and feet,
the crown and necklace of its jaws and teeth
all spearing into the nape of my neck.
I dropped the hunting knife and the shooting stick.

The rest of the group had moved on ahead.
The blades and feathers of grasses and ferns
conducted something in the air, but time
was static, jammed shut. Nerves strained with the sense

of a trap half-sprung, a pin almost pulled,
and all noise was a tight thread stretched and thinned
to breaking point and blood in its circuit
awaited a pulse. The turnpike of a branch
bent slowly back to shape across the trail.
Up high, a treetop craned its weather vane;
a storm-cloud split and it started to rain.
I was shouldered home in the fibreglass tomb
of a yellow canoe. Then sat up straight—
alive. Unharmed, in fact. In fact untouched.

I've heard it said that a human face
shaved in the hairs on the back of a head
can stop a jaguar dead in its tracks,
the way a tattoo of Christ, crucified
across the shoulder blades and down the spine,
in past times, could save a thief from the lash.
Years on, nothing has changed. I'm still the man
to be hauled down, ripped apart, but a sharp
backward glance, as it were, is all it takes.
I sense it mostly in the day-to-day:
not handling some rare gem or art object
but flicking hot fat over a bubbling egg,
test-flying a stunt-kite from Blackstone Edge,
not swearing to tell the whole truth on oath
but bending to read the meter with a torch,
tonguing the seamless flux of a gold tooth,
not shaking the hands of serial killers
but dead-heading dogwood with secateurs,
eyeballing blue tits through binoculars,
not crossing the great ocean by pedalo
but moseying forward in the middle lane,
hanging wallpaper flush to the plumb-line,

not barrelling over sky-high waterfalls
but brass-rubbing the hallmarks of fob-watches,
lying on top of sex, in the afterwards,
not metal-detecting the beach for land-mines
but tilting the fins of pinball machines,
pencilling snidey comments in the margins,
not escaping into freedom or peacetime
but trousering readies extruded from cashpoints,
eating the thick air that blasts the escarpment,
not rising to the bait of a fur coat
but yacking on the cordless, cruising Ceefax,
checking the pollen-count and long-range forecast,
not whipping up the mother-of-all soufflés
but picking off clay pipes with an air-rifle
at the side-show, describing myself as
white in the tick-box, dipping the dipstick,
needling pips from half a pomegranate,
not cranking up the system to overload
but licking the Christian Aid envelope,
lining up a family photograph,
not chasing twisters across Oklahoma
but changing a flat tyre on the hard shoulder,
dousing for C4 with a coat hanger,
not carving a slice from the Golden Calf
but hiking the town's municipal golf course,
drowning an inner tube in a horse trough,
not feeling the sonic boom bodily
but swiping a key card in the hotel lobby,
easing up for the lollipop lady,
not inhabiting the divine sepulchre,
not crowing over Arctic adventure,
not standing gob-smacked beneath ancient sculpture,
not kneeling empty-handed, open-mouthed

at the altar, but in the barber's chair
or tattoo parlour, in a sleepy trance,
catching in the mirror the startled face
of some scissor-hand, some needle-finger.

ROBINSON'S RESIGNATION

Because I am done with this thing called work,
the paper-clips and staples of it all.
The customers and their huge excuses,
their incredulous lies and their beautiful
foul-mouthed daughters. I am swimming with it,
right up to here with it. And I am bored,
bored like the man who married a mermaid.

And I am through with the business of work.
In meetings, with the minutes, I have dreamed
and doodled, drifted away then undressed
and dressed almost every single woman,
every button, every zip and buckle.
For eighteen months in this diving-helmet
I have lived with the stench of my own breath.

So I am finished with the whole affair.
As for this friendship thing, I couldn't give
a weeping fig for those so-called brothers
who are all voltage, no current. I have
emptied my locker. I should like to leave
and to fold things now like a pair of gloves
or two clean socks, one into the other.

This is my final word. Nothing will follow.

INCREDIBLE

After the first phase, after the great fall
between floorboards into the room below,
the soft landing, then standing one inch tall
within the high temple of table legs
or one inch long inside a matchbox bed . . .

And after the well-documented wars:
the tom-cat in its desert camouflage,
the spider in its chariot of limbs,
the sparrow in its single-seater plane . . .

After that, a new dominion of scale.
The earthrise of a final, human smile.
The pure inconsequence of nakedness,
the obsolescence of flesh and bone.
Every atom ballooned. Those molecules
that rose as billiard balls went by as moons.
Neutrinos dawned and bloomed, each needle's eye
became the next cathedral door, flung wide.

So yardsticks, like pit-props, buckled and failed.

Lifetimes went past. With the critical mass
of hardly more than the thought of a thought
I kept on, headlong, to vanishing point.
I looked for an end, for some dimension
to hold hard and resist. But I still exist.

A NOTE ABOUT THE AUTHOR

Simon Armitage is Professor of Poetry at the University of Sheffield, United Kingdom, and has written extensively for radio and television. His previous titles include *Kid, Book of Matches, The Dead Sea Poems, CloudCuckooLand, Killing Time, The Universal Home Doctor, Homer's Odyssey, Tyrannosaurus Rex Versus the Corduroy Kid,* and *Seeing Stars*. His many honors include a Forward Poetry Prize, and the Sunday Times Young Writer of the Year Award. His acclaimed translation of *Sir Gawain and the Green Knight* was published in 2007, and in 2010 he received the CBE for services to poetry.

A NOTE ON THE TYPE

The text of this book was set in Bembo, a facsimile of a typeface cut by Francesco Griffo for Aldus Manutius, the celebrated Venetian printer, in 1495. The face was named for Pietro Cardinal Bembo, the author of the small treatise entitled *De Aetna* in which it first appeared. Through the research of Stanley Morison, it is now generally acknowledged that all oldstyle type designs up to the time of William Caslon can be traced to the Bembo cut.

The present-day version of Bembo was introduced by the Monotype Corporation of London in 1929. Sturdy, well-balanced, and finely proportioned, Bembo is a face of rare beauty and great legibility in all of its sizes.

Composed by North Market Street Graphics
Lancaster, Pennsylvania

Printed and bound by Thomson-Shore
Dexter, Michigan

Designed by Soonyoung Kwon